My Safety

By

Kirsty Holmes

©2018
Book Life
King's Lynn
Norfolk PE30 4LS

ISBN: 978-1-78637-218-5

All rights reserved
Printed in Malaysia

Written by:
Kirsty Holmes

Edited by:
Holly Duhig

Designed by:
Danielle Jones

A catalogue record for this book
is available from the British Library

Photo Credits

**Abbreviations: l-left, r-right, b-bottom,
t-top, c-centre, m-middle.**

Contents

Words that look like **this** can be found in the glossary on page 24.

Staying Safe

Look around you. What exciting things can you see?

The world is very interesting. There are so many things to look at and places to explore!

Accidents

If you have a small accident, you might just need a plaster.

If we find something that isn't safe, we can get hurt. This is called an accident.

At Home

Always let a grown-up help you in the kitchen.

Home is a safe place. We still need to be **careful** with some things, though.

Don't fall down the stairs! Use the rail, or hold someone's hand.

Never touch a plug socket!

Plug sockets can give you an **electric shock**. This can be a bad accident to have.

10

Pets love a cuddle. Never hurt them, or they might bite or scratch you.

Always be kind to animals, and they will be kind too!

Always wear your helmet.

Falling off your bike or scooter can hurt. You could bump your knee or your head.

If you go swimming, always listen to a grown-up. It's important to be safe around water.

Special jackets can help you to float.

Holding hands keeps us safe.

Always stay with a grown-up when you are out shopping. It's easy to get lost.

Shop Assistant

Police Officer

Family

If you get lost, wait where you are.
Tell one of these people that you are lost.

Road Safety

Always cross the road with a grown-up. Never on your own.

Always look out for cars and other **vehicles** when you are out. Cars go very fast.

Before crossing the road, you must always stop, look, and listen for cars coming.

18

Seat belts **keep us safe.**
Don't undo them!

When you are in the car, you must sit in your car seat and keep your seat belt on.

Don't Touch!

Scissors

Medicine

Hot Drink

Iron

Many things look interesting, but aren't safe. If a grown-up tells you not to touch something, you must not touch it.

People Who Keep Us Safe

Parent

Doctor

Police Officer

Some people have the special job of looking after us. Do you know any of these people?

How do you think these people keep us safe? Talk about this with a grown-up.

Teacher

Firefighter

Lifeguard

Glossary

careful	making sure to avoid getting hurt
electric shock	an accident caused by electricity running through your body
float	to rest on and stay above water
hospital	a place where sick or injured people are cared for
seat belt	a strap designed to hold someone in a car seat
vehicles	things used for transporting people

Index